‖‖‖‖‖‖‖‖‖‖‖‖‖‖‖‖‖‖‖‖‖‖‖‖‖‖‖

☞ **W9-AVH-052**

ARCHIVED

ARCHIVED

ARCHIVED

TRUE OR FALSE?

This man can
read your mind.

TRUE!
(SORT OF)

Criss Angel is a magician who can make you believe he's reading your mind. But he doesn't claim to have ESP. He's a mentalist — somebody who can perform amazing mental tricks.

Some people claim that they really can read minds. Others say they can see into the future. These people are called psychics.

Do you believe in psychics? Lots of people do. But most scientists don't because nobody has ever been able to demonstrate that psychic powers are real. Read on to find out more about both sides of the psychic debate.

Book design Red Herring Design/NYC
Supervising editor: Jeffrey Nelson

Library of Congress Cataloging-in-Publication Data
Tilden, Thomasine E. Lewis.
Mind readers: science examines ESP / by Thomasine E. Lewis Tilden.
p. cm. — (24/7 : science behind the scenes)
Includes bibliographical references and index.
ISBN-13: 978-0-531-12075-0 (lib. bdg.)   978-0-531-17532-3 (pbk.)
ISBN-10: 0-531-12075-9 (lib. bdg.)   0-531-17532-4 (pbk.)
1. Extrasensory perception—Juvenile literature.
I. Title. II. Series.
BF1321.R838 2006
133.8—dc22   2006006781

32222000167033

© 2008 by Scholastic Inc.
All rights reserved. Published simultaneously in Canada. Printed in China. 62

FRANKLIN WATTS and associated logos are trademarks and/or registered trademarks of Scholastic Library Publishing. SCHOLASTIC and associated logos are trademarks and/or registered trademarks of Scholastic Inc.
6 7 8 9 10 R 17 16 15 14 13 12 11

MIND READERS

Science Examines ESP

Thomasine E. Lewis Tilden

WARNING: This book is about mind readers and other people with amazing mental powers. If people like these give you the creeps, read no further!

Franklin Watts
An Imprint of Scholastic Inc.
New York • Toronto • London • Auckland • Sydney
Mexico City • New Delhi • Hong Kong
Danbury, Connecticut

CONTENTS

ESP 411

Get the 411 on mind reading and other psychic powers.

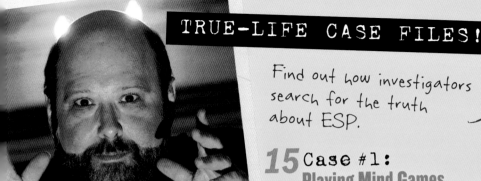

Find out how investigators search for the truth about ESP.

What's the secret behind this man's powers?

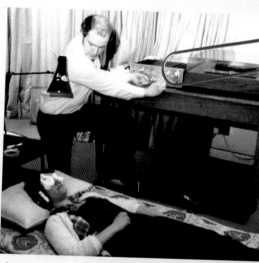

A researcher tests a woman to see whether she has ESP.

A psychic tracks three kids from New Jersey to Hawaii.

Find out more about people who claim to have ESP—and the researchers who are trying to find out whether it exists.

Most of us get information about the world through our five main senses—hearing, sight, touch, taste, and smell.

ESP 411

But some people say they have another way of getting information: through ESP, or extrasensory perception. Find out about this so-called "sixth sense"—and about the researchers who study it.

IN THIS SECTION:

- ▶ learn how ESP researchers talk;
- ▶ test your mind-reading skills;
- ▶ meet the people who investigate ESP.

Psychic-Speak

ESP researchers have their own way of talking. Find out what their vocabulary means.

How did you know the number I was thinking of? Do you have **ESP**?

ESP
(ee-ess-PEE) the ability to get information about the past, present, or future without using the five main senses. ESP stands for *extrasensory perception*.

psychic
(SYE-kik) somebody who claims to have ESP or other paranormal powers

No way. I think you're a **psychic**.

paranormal

(PAIR-uh-NOR-muhl) a term used to describe unusual events or abilities that can't be explained by science

mentalist

(MEN-tuh-list) a performer who uses tricks to make people think he or she has paranormal powers, such as the ability to read minds

> I don't have any **paranormal** powers. I'm a **mentalist**.

skeptic

(SKEP-tik) somebody who doubts or questions ideas or beliefs

telepathy

(teh-LEH-puh-thee) mind reading or mind-to-mind communication through ESP

> Actually, I'm a **skeptic**. I don't think anybody really has **telepathy**.

Say What?

Here's some more lingo.

psychokinesis (PK)

(sye-koh-kih-NEE-sis) the ability to use the mind to move or change objects
*She must have **PK**—the glass moved, even though she didn't touch it.*

parapsychologists

(PAIR-uh-sye-KOHL-uh-jists) researchers who study paranormal powers such as ESP and PK
*Some **parapsychologists** are convinced that ESP and PK really exist. Others are skeptical.*

pseudoscience

(SOO-doh-SYE-uhns) theories that appear to be based on science but aren't really scientific. *Pseudo means "false."*
*Many scientists think that parapsychology is a **pseudoscience**.*

sixth sense

(sixth sens) another term for ESP
*My **sixth sense** told me we'd bump into each other today.*

Are You a Mind Reader?

Use these Zener cards to find out.

The five images to the right are called **Zener cards**. As you can see, each has a different pattern. In a deck of Zener cards, there are five cards for each pattern.

In the 1930s, a researcher named Dr. J. B. Rhine used these cards to test people's ability to read minds. Now you can test your ESP, too.

▶ Make five copies of the Zener cards to create a deck of 25 cards. Shuffle them.
▶ Get a piece of paper and number it from 1 to 25.
▶ Find a partner. You'll be the "sender." Your partner is the "receiver." You'll be sending messages to your partner. Hopefully, he or she will be receiving them.
▶ Look at the first card. You should sit back-to-back so your partner can't see it. Try to communicate the pattern to your receiver just by thinking about it—in other words, by using telepathy.
▶ Ask your partner what pattern he or she thinks you're looking at.
▶ If the receiver chooses correctly, it's called a hit. If she doesn't, it's a miss.
▶ Record hits and misses on your paper.
▶ Continue until you've gone through all 25 cards.
▶ Add up the number of hits.

HOW MANY HITS?

On average, most receivers will get five out of 25 right. That's what you'd expect to get just by guessing. But Dr. Rhine found that some receivers got six or seven hits. Not just a few times—that could happen to anybody. But over and over.

Did that mean that these receivers had ESP?

Dr. Rhine thought so. For him, their high scores were proof that ESP was real.

But many scientists who examined his results disagreed. They saw problems in the way his test was designed. They found ways people could cheat. And they questioned his interpretation of the results.

Dr. Rhine claimed to have taken these criticisms into account when designing later experiments. And other tests for ESP have been designed since then. (See page 25.) But some parapsychologists still use Zener cards.

BACK TO MIND READING

Now switch places with your partner. Try to read your partner's mind. If you get more than five out of 25 right over and over, maybe you have ESP. Or maybe you're just lucky.

Opposite page: An ESP experiment with two young subjects in the 1950s. The sender (*at left*) tries to use telepathy to communicate Zener card patterns to the receiver (*at right*).

The Investigators

Some researchers look for evidence that ESP and psychokinesis exist. And some look for other ways to explain mysterious events.

STATISTICIANS
They are mathematicians who help psychologists and other scientists interpret the data they collect from their experiments.

PHYSICISTS
Physicists study things like matter (what things are made of) and energy. A few physicists have done experiments to find out whether it's possible to use the mind to move or change objects.

PSYCHOLOGISTS
They study behavior and the way the mind works. They try to understand why humans (and other animals) think and act the way they do.

PSYCHICS
They claim to have paranormal powers, such as the ability to see into the future, read minds, or change objects without touching them.

PARAPSYCHOLOGISTS
They are scientists who focus on the paranormal. Some believe that ESP and psychokinesis exist. Others are either open-minded or skeptical. But they all want to find out whether paranormal abilities are real.

MAGICIANS/ MENTALISTS
Some magicians and mentalists investigate claims of paranormal powers. Many of them believe that psychics use tricks to fool people into believing that they have amazing skills.

TRUE-LIFE

CASE FILES!

24 hours a day, 7 days a week, 365 days a year, researchers are trying to find out whether ESP really exists.

IN THIS SECTION:

- ▶ a mentalist convinces people that he can read their minds;

- ▶ studies show that ESP exists! Or maybe not;

- ▶ a psychic detective tracks down three missing kids.

A Guide to ESP

"You will fall off your bike tomorrow. . . . Better wear an old pair of jeans. . . ."

What would it be like to have ESP?

ESP stands for *extrasensory perception*. That's the ability to get information in some way other than through sight, hearing, or the other senses. Here are three types of ESP.

TYPE OF ESP: telepathy
DESCRIPTION: mind-to-mind communication
EXAMPLE: Imagine being able to send a mental text message to your friend in another class. You concentrate really hard on these words: *Meet you after school*. A minute later, you hear these words in your mind: *Can't. Got detention*.

TYPE OF ESP: clairvoyance
DESCRIPTION: the ability to see something that's happening out of sight. Telepathy involves information being sent from one mind to another. But clairvoyants claim to see things even though nobody is sending them information.
EXAMPLE: You're at school, and you get an image of smoke at your house. You call your mom. It turns out that she left something on the stove, and your call saves the house from burning down.

TYPE OF ESP: precognition
DESCRIPTION: the ability to know about something before it happens—to be able to see into the future. (*Pre* means "before" and *cognition* has to do with knowledge.)
EXAMPLE: You have a quick flash of your friend getting stitches. And the next day he falls off his bike and has to have the cut on his knee sewn up.

Playing
Mind Games

Marc Salem says he has no psychic powers. And yet he's one of the world's greatest mind readers.

Mental Magic

Marc Salem dazzles audiences with his mind-reading powers.

Unbelievable! Miraculous!! Mind-blowing!!!

These are the words audiences use to describe Marc Salem.

Salem has entertained people around the world with his show "Mind Games." His performance makes people laugh. It also makes them think. But mostly it makes them wonder, *How in the world did he do that?*

Salem wows his audiences by seeming to read their minds. He asks people to pick words out of a book and think about them. Then he tells them what those words are. He also picks volunteers and asks some of them to lie to him. Then he picks out who the liars are. He's never wrong.

Salem asks people to write numbers on a pad. Somebody adds up the numbers. Then Salem plays a taped message in which he announces what the sum of the numbers is. And he recorded the message *earlier* that day! The audience gasps.

How does Salem do it? Does he really have ESP?

Marc Salem's ability to read minds has amazed millions of people. Some say he must be psychic, but Salem denies that he can really read minds.

Unusual Powers

As a kid, Marc used to try to read his brother's mind. He often seemed to succeed.

When Marc was a kid, his parents noticed that he seemed to have unusual powers. He could always guess what gift he was getting for Hanukkah. And he often knew where the family was going on vacation ahead of time.

One day, Marc and his brother were playing at a creek. "I told him we had to leave, that there were snakes there," Salem says. His brother looked around; there were no snakes. A few days later, though, the area was crawling with snakes.

Marc also tried to read his brother's mind. They would sit in a dark room and Marc would ask his brother to think of a number. Then Marc would try to guess it. Often he was right.

As a child, Salem could often tell what people were thinking. He says it's because he picked up on nonverbal cues.

In high school, Marc's powers seemed even sharper. He discovered that he could tell when people were lying. He learned to recognize the expressions and gestures people make when they're not telling the truth.

Marc had always been fascinated by how the mind works. He was also interested in how people communicate, especially in nonverbal ways. So in college and graduate school, he studied **psychology**, the study of human behavior and how the mind works.

At the same time, Marc began performing a show in which he demonstrated his mind-reading skills. He was on his way to becoming one of the most famous mentalists in the world.

A Human Lie Detector

Salem uses his skills to help police officers fight crime—and to win a worldwide audience.

After finishing graduate school, Marc Salem took his one-man show on the road. Audiences around the world were amazed by his ability to tell what people were thinking. He also impressed them with his skills as a human lie detector.

He was so good at identifying liars that he caught the attention of a former police commissioner who came to the show. Soon, Salem was offered a job teaching police officers how to tell whether someone is lying.

Salem thinks it's almost impossible for a liar to fool him. He says there are physical signs that give a liar away. You just have to know what to look for.

Some people who see Salem's show think that

he has helpers in the audience or uses hidden cameras. But Salem denies it. He says that he uses only his own skills as a magician. And he has offered to pay $100,000 to anyone who can prove that he relies on anything but his talent.

On May 25, 2005, *60 Minutes*, a TV news show, did a story about Salem. It was hosted by a well-known reporter, Mike Wallace. The taping took place in a theater in New York City. To make sure Salem had no helpers in the theater, *60 Minutes* picked the audience. As the taping began, Wallace admitted that he was skeptical about Salem's skills. But by the end of the show, he had changed his mind.

Salem has performed his show *Mind Games* all over the world. How does he explain his success? He says he watches people closely and picks up information from gestures and expressions.

Focus on My Forehead

Salem starts the show by reading Wallace's mind.

Wallace joined Salem on stage, and the show began. Salem asked Wallace to pick three books from a pile on a table. Salem fanned the pages of one book and told Wallace to stop him at any page.

In 2005, Salem appeared on the TV show *60 Minutes*. To make sure he had no helpers in the theater, the show's producers picked the audience.

"Look at the first couple of words on the page and lock them in your mind," he said to Wallace. Then he told him to shut the book.

"I want you to stare at my forehead," Salem said. "It's easy to do. It goes to the back of my neck." The audience laughed. Salem is bald.

"See the first letter of the word you're thinking of," Salem continued. "Just focus on the letter." He paused. "Is that an *a*?" he asked.

"Yes, it is," Wallace answered, shaking his head in amazement.

"Is the next letter an *l*?" Once again, Wallace said yes. "The next letter is also an *l*," Salem said. Correct again. The letters spelled *all*—the very word Wallace had chosen!

Salem handed the next book to a woman in the front row. He asked her to select a word from it, focus on it, and stare at his forehead. He correctly guessed the first few letters and then asked her whether the word was *photographer*. She nodded, and the audience gasped.

Next, Salem asked for four people to come up on stage. He told Wallace and each of the volunteers to do a sketch on a big white card. He couldn't see what they were drawing.

Salem asked a volunteer to mix the cards up and hand a card back to each person. Now they all held a card that had either their own drawing on it or someone

else's. "When I ask if that's your drawing, no matter if it is or not, you answer, *No*," Salem told them.

While blindfolded, Salem guessed the serial number on a dollar bill Mike Wallace (*right*) handed him.

One by one, he asked them, "Is that your drawing?" And each answered, "No." Salem then correctly picked out those who were telling the truth and those who were lying.

Then he asked Wallace for a dollar bill. Still blindfolded, Salem touched the bill and rattled off its long serial number. Wallace looked shocked. How did he do it?

Is it possible, Wallace wondered, that Salem possesses some kind of paranormal ability? It certainly seems that way. But Salem doesn't claim to be a psychic. "I don't even know what a psychic is," he told Wallace. So how does he explain his amazing skills?

21

"Reading" People

Salem picks up signals from a person's body language and tone of voice.

Salem believes that words are only a small part of how people communicate. "[Most] of the information we **convey** is not what we say, but how we say it," he explains. A person's tone of voice says a lot about what he's thinking. Facial expressions and gestures also reveal a lot.

Salem says that people can learn to read these nonverbal signals by developing their powers of observation. He has trained himself to look and listen carefully. Would you notice if somebody looked away or cleared his throat before answering a question? Salem would. Those are things people often do if they're hiding something.

But how does Salem explain his other skills? For example, when he was a kid, how was he able to guess which numbers his brother was thinking of?

Salem says that knowing the way his brother's mind worked helped him

Facial expressions and gestures like these give Salem clues to what a person is thinking.

predict the numbers he would pick. Today, when Salem asks his wife to think of a color, he usually knows which color she will choose. "It happens the more you do this with someone you're close to," Salem says. "You are not reading their thoughts. You are seeing the world from their eyes."

What about the snakes at the creek? Salem says that he was just observant. He must have noticed holes in the ground and figured there were snakes living there.

Okay, fine. But how does he explain being able to correctly guess the word Wallace was thinking of? Or knowing the numbers on the dollar bill?

He doesn't. "I am a mentalist, not a psychic," is all he will say. And mentalists, like magicians, don't reveal their secrets. "We have to keep the mystery," Salem says. 24/7

PICK A NUMBER

Here's a simple mind-reading trick: Ask a friend to pick a number from one to four. Then, when you read her mind, tell her she picked the number three. Chances are you're right. Why? Because you already said "one" and "four," and the word *to* sounds like two. So she picked the only number you didn't mention.

TRAINING YOUR
EYES AND EARS

How can you tell whether someone is lying? Here are Marc Salem's tips for reading body language and tone of voice.

PAY ATTENTION to posture, gestures, and facial expressions. You can pick up a lot of information by observing how people move and express themselves.

CONCENTRATE on *how* people talk, not just what they say. Their tone, choice of words, pauses, and even silences reveal a lot. If somebody's voice cracks, that may be a sign he's lying. Or maybe he just has a cold. To know whether the crack in his voice means anything, you have to use the final skill . . .

TRANSLATION. That's Salem's word for interpretation. You need to compare and judge what you see and hear. For example, do the gestures and vocal tone match? Maybe a person sounds calm but her gestures indicate nervousness. That could mean she's hiding something.

"[People] are always giving off information," Salem says. "The question is: Are you receptive enough to pick it up?"

Marc Salem says he doesn't have telepathy. But what about the people who claim to have ESP? Does it really exist? Researchers are conducting tests to find out. Read on to learn what they've discovered.

Laboratories worldwide
1880s-present

Do You See What I See?

Investigators claim their tests show that ESP is real. But many scientists question their results.

Testing for ESP

Since the 1880s, researchers have been testing subjects for the ability to read minds.

You're sitting in a big, comfortable chair. You put on headphones and hear a quiet hum that drowns out all other sounds.

A researcher finishes preparations for a Ganzfeld test.

Red light fills the room. You lean back in your chair, and a researcher puts half of a ping-pong ball over each of your eyes. You can see a faint red glow through them.

Welcome to the Ganzfeld experiment. It's a way for researchers to test whether telepathy is real—whether someone can actually read another person's mind.

In the Ganzfeld experiment, researchers remove all the bright and loud things that usually distract you. Your five main senses get to take a nap. Now maybe your "sixth" sense—ESP—can get to work.

Sitting in a room nearby is a sender. That's the person who's trying to send you messages—without saying a word.

Your job is to try to receive these messages.

You feel relaxed, and your mind is blank. You begin to describe whatever you see in your mind. That's what the researcher instructed you to do. She's in another room, listening to and recording everything you say.

What images are you seeing? Are they anything like the ones the sender is seeing?

Meanwhile, in Another Room . . .

The sender tries to communicate with the receiver.

Down the hall, the sender is looking at a picture or short video clip. That's called the "target." Let's say that the sender is looking at a video of a storm at sea.

You have never met this person. And since he's sitting in a soundproof room, there's no way the two of you can cheat.

The sender tries to silently communicate what he's seeing—huge waves, dark clouds, a boat being tossed about. He also tries to share what he feels as he watches—awe at the storm's power, fear for the people in the boat.

At the same time, you're describing what you're seeing in your mind. At first, you see a kid chewing gum and blowing a bubble. But that doesn't last long. That image is replaced by an image of a beach. People are playing in the surf. You see something moving out in the water. It's a surfer, and he's riding a big wave . . .

The Moment of Truth

You look at four images and then make your choice. What does it mean if you pick the target?

The **session** lasts for half an hour. Then you meet with the researcher. She shows you four different pictures or video clips. One of them is the target. You study all four, and then you give each one a score. You give the highest score to the one that is most similar to what you were seeing.

If you give the highest score to the target, it's counted as a hit. But if you score one of the other images higher, it's a miss.

You remember that you saw big waves during your session. So you give the video of the storm the highest score. You get a hit! You didn't see the same thing as the sender, but you picked the target. That counts as a positive result.

Still, that doesn't mean that you have telepathy. You had four images to choose from, so you had a one in four, or 25 percent, chance of guessing which one was the target.

After attempting to receive images using ESP, a subject looks for the image that is most similar to what she had visualized.

But let's say 100 people take part in a study, and 50 of them pick the target. In other words, their overall score is 50 percent. That's a lot higher than the 25 percent score you'd expect if they were just guessing. Does that high score mean that some of them have telepathy?

TUNED IN

One study of 20 young dancers, musicians, and actors had amazing results. Seventy-five percent of the musicians picked the target! Are musicians better than other people at tuning in ESP signals? Or was the sample too small to mean anything?

Not necessarily. Parapsychologists don't think the results of one study mean anything. But if the overall score of *many* studies were 50 percent, that would be convincing evidence that telepathy is real.

In fact, when researchers combined the scores of Ganzfeld studies done from the 1970s through the 1990s, they came up with an overall hit rate of 34 percent. The score was based on dozens of studies involving hundreds of people. Parapsychologists were excited by the results. For them, a 34 percent hit rate was evidence that ESP exists.

Still, skeptics weren't convinced.

Who's Right?

Does the evidence show that ESP is real? Parapsychologists and skeptics disagree.

Skeptics say that the Ganzfeld experiments haven't really demonstrated anything. If ESP exists, they say, ESP researchers would get the same high results each time the experiment is done. But in the Ganzfeld studies, some investigators had positive results, while others didn't. To demonstrate that a **theory** is correct, the skeptics say, different researchers have to do the same experiment and get similar results.

Say, for example, you wanted to investigate whether gravity exists—whether there's a force that pulls things toward Earth and keeps them from floating into space. As an experiment, you could drop objects of different weights. You'd expect them all to fall to the ground, and of course they would. You could ask all your friends to do the same experiment—and they'd get the same results.

Then you could be confident stating that gravity is a real force. But what if objects sometimes went up instead of down when you dropped them? Wouldn't that make you doubt the law of gravity? That's how most scientists feel about telepathy. If it really exists, they say, each study would demonstrate evidence of it.

Skeptics also questioned how the Ganzfeld

tests were conducted. In early tests, researchers sometimes knew what the target was. Were they able to influence a receiver's choice? In other cases, the sender and receiver were friends. Did that affect the outcomes?

A woman takes part in a Ganzfeld experiment. In early tests, were receivers accidentally given information about the target images?

Parapsychologists listened to the skeptics' criticism and made changes in the way the experiments were conducted. But even after the testing methods were improved, skeptics still questioned the way the results were interpreted.

So where does that leave us? In 1970, paranormal investigator Milbourne Christopher said: "[Researchers] have yet to find a single person who can, without trickery, send or receive even a three-letter word under test conditions." After dozens of Ganzfeld studies, has anything changed?

Robert Morris believed that the studies offered solid evidence of ESP. Until 2004, he was the director of the Koestler Institute in Scotland, where some of those studies took place. He said that the tests made him 90 percent sure that "something is going on."

Dr. Susan Blackmore came to a different conclusion. She is a well-known parapsychologist. At least, she *was*. She spent years searching for evidence that ESP was real. But in 2000, Blackmore finally gave up. "I am a scientist," she says. "I think the way to truth is by investigation. I suspect that telepathy [and other paranormal powers] do not exist because I have been looking in vain for them for 25 years."

There is one thing parapsychologists and their critics agree on: more studies are needed. And if in the future anybody demonstrates that ESP is real, Blackmore would be "back like a shot." She knows it would be one of the biggest scientific discoveries of all time.

But she's not holding her breath. 24/7

A PRIZEWINNING DISCOVERY?

If anyone ever demonstrates that ESP is real, scientists will be happy to recognize their achievement. As Richard Dawkins, a well-known biologist, puts it: "The discoverer of a new energy field that links mind to mind in telepathy . . . deserves a Nobel Prize." But Dawkins points out that paranormal abilities "have a habit of going away whenever they're tested." In other words, he doesn't believe they exist.

Nancy Weber:
Psychic Detective

Three kids are missing, and the police have no leads. Can a psychic detective find them?

This case study is true, but the names of the family members involved have been changed to protect their privacy.

Three Missing Kids

A mother comes to pick up her kids. But their father has kidnapped them.

Debbie Keyes pulled up in front of her ex-husband's house in Harding, New Jersey. It was March 20, 1980. She was coming to pick up her children, who had been staying with their dad. But when she entered the house, the rooms were bare. The closets were empty. And her children were gone.

Keyes made a **frantic** call to 911. "My children!" she screamed. "They're gone!"

Within minutes, a police officer arrived. Keyes told him that she and her husband, Buddy, were divorced. They had been fighting over **custody** of the children—who would have the right to keep them. A judge had decided that the children should live with her, and she had come to pick them up.

Now her three kids—eight-year-old Callie, seven-year-old Kristen, and four-year-old Jason—were gone. Her ex-husband had taken them, and Keyes had no idea where they could be.

Debbie Keyes called 911 to report her missing children. An operator immediately sent a police officer to the scene.

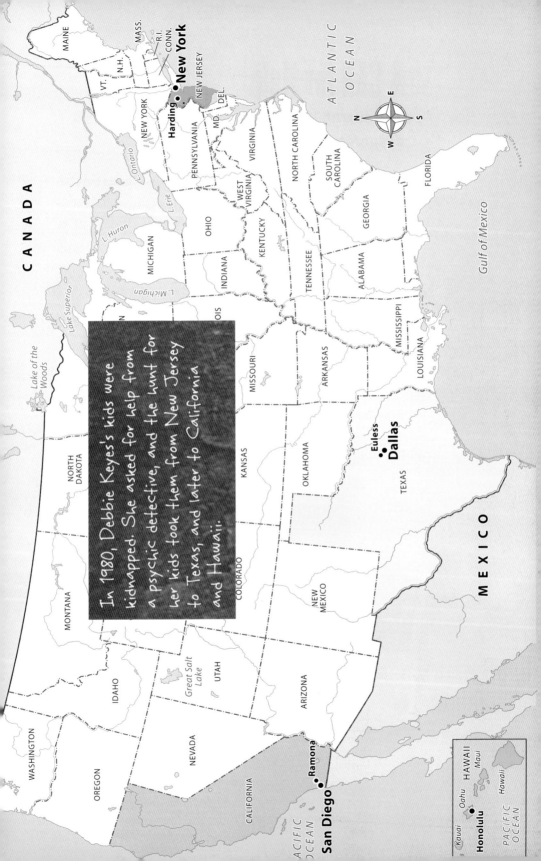

In 1980, Debbie Keyes's kids were kidnapped. She asked for help from a psychic detective, and the hunt for her kids took them from New Jersey to Texas, and later to California and Hawaii.

A Call for Help

The search leads nowhere. So Keyes makes a desperate call.

Detective Lou Masterbone was assigned to the case. He immediately ordered an all-points bulletin (APB) on Buddy Keyes. The police throughout the area would now be on the lookout for a man with three young kids. Buddy Keyes was a wanted man.

Weeks passed with no reported sightings of the children or their dad. Keyes knew that her children could be anywhere.

After several months, Masterbone still had no leads. Then one day, Keyes was driving around town, putting up flyers about her missing children. As she drove, Keyes listened to the radio. A psychic named Nancy Weber was being interviewed. She was talking about how she helped the police find missing people.

Maybe she can help me, thought Keyes. She had never gone to a psychic in her life, but she was desperate. "I would do anything to look for the kids," she explained later.

She decided to give Weber a call.

Debbie Keyes put up many flyers like this one. But nobody reported seeing her children.

MISSING CHILD
Missing

A Psychic Detective

Nancy Weber says she's psychic. She uses her special powers to help people.

Even as a child, Nancy Weber felt she had special powers. She says she saw things that other people couldn't see. When she was 15, she told her older sister, who was pregnant, that she would give birth the next day at 2:56 P.M. She said the baby would be a boy who weighed 7 pounds and 11 ounces (3.5 kg).

Nancy Weber has been working as a psychic for more than 30 years.

The next day, Weber says, her sister gave birth at 2:56 in the afternoon to a boy who weighed 7 pounds and 11 ounces!

The doctor heard about Weber's prediction and said she must be a witch. Comments like that convinced Weber to keep her skills secret.

For many years, Weber worked as a nurse. In 1975, she began giving psychic readings, and soon became a full-time psychic and healer.

Weber also began working with the police. Detectives sometimes turned to her for help with difficult cases.

When Keyes called and told Weber her story, the psychic felt she had to try to help. She agreed to meet. She asked Keyes to bring pictures of the kids and some of their belongings.

Weber "Sees" the Children

The psychic's vision leads the police to Texas. But are the kids really there?

Nancy Weber greeted Debbie Keyes and said they should take a walk. As they walked, Weber held the kids' belongings and looked at the photos Keyes had brought. "Let me just see what I see," she told Keyes.

"When I look at a photo, there comes this moment where I know I'm making contact with this person," Weber explains. As she studied the pictures, she began to feel tense. Suddenly she saw an image of the children with their father. She felt that the dad had a bad temper, and Keyes said that was true. But Weber said that the children were safe.

"Can you tell me where they are?" Keyes asked.

"Let me see if something comes to me," Weber said, closing her eyes. A moment later she said, "Texas," and asked to see a map.

"Once I opened the map, I felt pulled, like a magnet," Weber says. She pointed to a town on the map and said, "I see them in Euless, Texas."

Keyes was excited to finally have a location where the police could look for her kids. But first she had to convince Masterbone to take the psychic seriously. "My reaction was, are you nuts?" he said later. "So I called a couple of . . .

police officers who had used Weber before. And they said, yes, they would recommend her."

The detective called the school system in Euless and was shocked to learn that the two girls were enrolled in school there. "I almost fell out of my chair," Masterbone told a CNN interviewer later. With the whole country to choose from, Weber had pinpointed the kids' exact location!

The Euless school board gave Masterbone the kids' address, and he contacted the local police. But when the cops got to the address, they found an empty apartment. Buddy Keyes and his children had disappeared again.

After Weber "saw" the missing children in a suburb of Dallas, Texas, the detective found out that they were enrolled in a school there!

PSYCHIC OR FRAUD?

This man fouled up the search for a serial killer.

Since 1962, a serial killer had been preying on women in Boston, Massachusetts. The murderer, known as the Boston Strangler, was terrorizing the city.

In 1964, the state attorney general, Edward Brooke, took over the investigation. He formed a task force that would be called the Strangler Bureau. And he also decided to call in a world-famous psychic, Peter Hurkos, for help. Hurkos said he'd gained his psychic powers after a fall from a ladder. He claimed to have solved countless murders.

Hurkos worked by holding objects that had once belonged to the victims. He said he received "vibrations" from these objects that gave him clues about a case.

In Boston, Hurkos gave the police detailed and accurate descriptions of crime scenes where the Strangler's victims had been found. These descriptions convinced many in the Strangler Bureau that Hurkos had real psychic powers. So when Hurkos came up with a description of the suspect, the police made an arrest based on his visions.

But the suspect was innocent.

Psychic Peter Hurkos described his powers this way: "I see pictures in my mind like on a TV screen."

Was Hurkos a Fraud?

A few months later, Hurkos was arrested for impersonating an FBI agent. Critics called Hurkos a fraud. They claimed that he often pretended to be a detective so he could get inside information about crimes. That's how he made himself seem psychic.

No one ever proved that Hurkos received inside information about the Strangler murders. Still, the incident badly damaged the reputation of the Strangler Bureau. The group was accused of wasting valuable time working with a fraud.

The real Boston Strangler was arrested later that year.

Ten Months Later

With no breaks in the case, Masterbone and Keyes turn to Weber for a second time.

Ten months passed with no breaks in the case. Finally, Keyes and Masterbone decided to ask Weber for help again. This time, Weber said she felt herself being pulled farther west. She could smell the ocean and hear waves. "California," she said suddenly. "They're in California."

They were in a town whose name began with the letter *R*, she said. She saw a street sign, but it was just a single letter. "E Street," she said. "In . . . *Ramona*, California."

Masterbone had a feeling that Weber was right again. So he flew to California. In Ramona, he and a local policeman walked house-to-house on E Street. Amazingly, they found a man who recognized a photo of the kids. He was their neighbor. Weber had been right again!

The news wasn't all good. The neighbor said that the family had moved to Hawaii a few days earlier. But luckily, he had their new address. Within a few days, the police in Hawaii had arrested Buddy Keyes, and the children were reunited with their mother. They had been apart for 13 months.

Keyes was stunned that Weber had been able to locate the kids

Thanks to Weber's help, Debbie Keyes and her children were finally reunited in Honolulu, Hawaii.

41

from thousands of miles away. "I never thought I would find them." Keyes said later. "Nancy gave me hope and courage. Everything she said came true. It was absolutely amazing."

Psychics and the Police

There have been some success stories. But most police chiefs are skeptical of psychics.

How did Weber know that the children had been in Texas and California? Did she really "see" them in those places? People who believe in psychics would say yes.

But skeptics think there must be some other explanation. Could Weber have noticed details that others missed? Did she have any other knowledge of the case that might have helped her?

It's impossible to know for sure. Whatever Weber did, Debbie Keyes was very grateful to her for finding her children. But usually cases involving psychics don't have such happy endings. And most police forces in the country won't work with them.

Most police chiefs say that psychics often give investigators bad information. Sometimes, when a crime happens, several psychics will call the cops with tips. But usually they offer conflicting information. Then the police have to figure out whether any of the leads are worth looking into. Often they ignore them all.

In 1979, the Los Angeles Police Department conducted a study with 12 psychics. The psychics were given details about four cases and asked to provide leads. But the leads they provided were of little or no use to the police. The researchers concluded that there was no evidence that psychics could help in criminal investigations.

The studies convinced the FBI—the Federal Bureau of Investigation—that psychics could not provide their agents with useful information. So the agency forbids FBI agents to use psychics in their investigations.

Still, sometimes psychics *do* help investigations. Weber certainly did. And Masterbone gives her credit for solving the case. "If it wasn't for Nancy, we never would have gotten those children back," he says. "She was the key to the whole puzzle." 24/7

The headquarters of the Federal Bureau of Investigation (FBI) in Washington, D.C. The bureau doesn't allow psychics to work with its agents.

HOW DO THEY DO IT?

Two writers say that many psychic detectives use the same skills as other detectives.

Is it possible that Weber is just a good detective? That's what Marcello Truzzi and Arthur Lyons would probably say. They wrote a book called *The Blue Sense: Psychic Detectives and Crime*.

Truzzi and Lyons believe that many psychic detectives use the same skills as real detectives. They observe people closely and listen carefully. They pick up on clues that others might miss. They use their powers of **deduction**, and also know when to follow through on **hunches**.

The writers also say that psychics do a lot of guessing. Sometimes psychics throw out lots of information, hoping that some of it will fit the case. If one guess turns out to be right, people forget all the wrong guesses.

A Body in the Woods

Psychics also provide vague information. They'll say, "I see trees" or "I see water." Or they'll predict something they know

has a good chance of being true. For example, a psychic may "see" a body in the woods—but that's where many murder victims are found.

Psychics may also get better press than they deserve. Let's say a psychic detective works on ten cases but only gives good information on one. That's the case the public will hear about.

Of course, some psychic detectives are just con artists. But Truzzi and Lyons say that many psychics honestly believe that they have special powers. And the writers don't rule out the possibility that some of them really might have ESP.

The famous fictional detective Sherlock Holmes (*right*) often amazed his assistant, Dr. Watson (*left*), with his keen powers of observation and deduction. Do psychics use those same skills to solve crimes?

ESP DOWNLOAD

Find out more about people who claim to have ESP or PK— and those who investigate them.

Mid-1800s
They Talk to Dead People

The Fox sisters of New York claim to have psychic powers. One is the ability to move objects using only the power of their minds. Another is the ability to contact the dead. The belief that **mediums** can talk with the dead starts a new religious movement called **Spiritualism**. Its popularity leads to a growing interest in the paranormal.

Key Dates in Psychic History

Ever since psychics became popular in the 1800s, researchers have been investigating their claims.

1882 A Scientific Approach

The Society for Psychical Research is formed in London. It's the first group to use scientific methods to investigate psychic experiences.

1920s Exposing Fakes

Magician Harry Houdini believes that mediums and psychics are fooling people. His experience as a magician allows him to reveal the tricks they use. He exposes many famous mediums.

1927 A Wonder Horse

Psychic researchers claim that a horse named Lady Wonder (*right*) has telepathy. A spectator thinks of a word, and the horse spells it out by choosing panels with letters on them. But a magician figures out that Lady Wonder's trainer uses secret signals to guide the "mind-reading" horse.

1930s Testing ESP in the Lab

Dr. Joseph Banks Rhine invents the terms *ESP* and *parapsychology*. He and his wife create the Parapsychology Laboratory at Duke University. Researchers there use Zener cards to test people for ESP. Rhine announces that the experiments show that ESP is both real and common.

1970s A Psychic Superstar

Uri Geller (*right*) becomes famous for bending spoons using only the power of his mind. But skeptics say that he uses tricks. So they're not surprised when Geller appears on a popular TV show and is unable to bend spoons provided by the producers.

1976 The Need for Skepticism

A group of scientists and journalists form a group that's now called the Committee for Skeptical Inquiry. Its goals are to promote critical thinking and to make people aware of bad or fake science. (Their magazine is shown here.)

Psychics in the News

Scientists Try to Solve Mind-Bending Mystery!

Imagine being able to move or change an object without touching it. That power is called psychokinesis (PK), and psychologist John Palmer thinks that some people really have it.

Palmer works at the Rhine Research Center in Raleigh-Durham, North Carolina. His research focuses on people who seem to create movement or sound in an unexplained way.

"It usually involves a young person around the age of puberty having some sort of emotional problems at home," Palmer says. "Most of the time the individual claims that they are not trying to make these things happen. But they are happening. A chair might turn over; light switches go on and off; things fall off a table."

Some famous psychics have claimed to have PK. One of them was Uri Geller. He was a psychic superstar who was often on TV in the 1960s and 1970s. He said he could bend spoons using the power of his mind. Geller would hold a spoon and gently rub it, and then it would start to bend.

Most researchers who tested Geller

Geller claimed he could bend spoons and stop clocks with the power of his mind.

found no evidence that he had special powers. But a few concluded that he did have PK. Still, skeptics found many flaws in their research. Magician James Randi said that Geller simply used the same tricks as other magicians. "If Uri Geller bends spoons with divine powers, then he's doing it the hard way," Randi joked.

Geller no longer does his spoon-bending act. "I got away from that a long time ago," he says.

How do researchers study PK? Palmer starts by interviewing witnesses who have seen it happen.

"It's like investigating a crime scene," he says. Then, when possible, he tries to bring people into a lab "to attempt to show PK under controlled conditions."

Palmer can't explain how PK works. "It might be a type of energy coming from the person," Palmer says. "All we know is that things move and the person isn't exerting any physical energy to move the objects. It is difficult to draw firm conclusions. It's an unsolved mystery. What we're doing is trying to solve it."

Author Predicts *Titanic* Sinking!

She was the biggest ship ever built, and her designer said she was unsinkable. But in 1912, on her first voyage, the *Titanic* hit an iceberg and sank.

The tragic news saddened people around the world. But it may not have surprised a man named Morgan Robertson. Fourteen years earlier, Robertson had written a novel about a huge ship called the *Titan*. In his book, the *Titan* hit an iceberg and sank!

Today, some people see this incident as evidence that Robertson had a form of ESP called precognition. They say that he may have actually seen into the future.

But does Robertson's book actually prove that he was psychic—or that psychic powers are real? No, the experts say, that would take controlled scientific experiments, with repeated measurable results.

Still, it was certainly an eerie coincidence. . . .

Did one man foresee the sinking of the *Titanic*?   49

Kid Claims She's Psychic!

NEW YORK, NEW YORK—February 1, 2002

Natalia Lulova came to Manhattan yesterday with a simple goal: to win $1 million. All she had to do was convince magician James Randi that she was psychic. If she passed his test, Natalia would become a millionaire.

Randi—also known as the Amazing Randi—spends much of his time investigating claims of paranormal powers. He says he wants to reveal the tricks so-called psychics use to fool the public. He has uncovered many hoaxes and frauds.

Randi is sure that psychic abilities don't exist. To prove his point, he has offered to pay $1 million to anybody who can demonstrate his or her paranormal ability in a test. Many people have accepted his challenge. But they all failed to win the prize.

Natalia was sure she would be the first to pass Randi's test.

An Amazing Claim

In 2001, Randi received a call from a lawyer representing Natalia, who was ten at the time. He claimed that Natalia could sense colors and read words from cards placed in front of her "with her eyes totally covered with a piece of black cloth."

The lawyer said that Natalia wanted to accept Randi's "One Million Dollar Paranormal Challenge." Randi agreed, and he and the lawyer decided on rules for the test. One rule was that Natalia would take the test twice. The first time, somebody on Natalia's team would put on her blindfold. The second time, Randi would blindfold her. Natalia had to succeed both times in order to win the prize.

The Big Day Arrives

Natalia's mother, lawyer, and coach accompanied her to the meeting with Randi. Her coach is a Russian engineer who helps people develop their paranormal powers. Natalia's family **emigrated** from Russia three years ago, and they now live in Brooklyn, New York.

Natalia's coach placed the blindfold on Natalia. It was made of two foam pads covered in black fabric. Natalia

Natalia Lulova was sure she would win Randi's $1 million prize.

adjusted it a little and said she was ready.

For the next seven minutes, Natalia read from a book, picked words written on cards, and identified colors. She even played tic-tac-toe with her coach and beat him.

Now it was Randi's turn. He replaced her blindfold with a pair of swimming goggles. The lenses were covered by silver foil and filled with pieces of sponge. He put tape across the bridge of her nose and around the edges of the goggles. He also asked her not to rub or pull on her face.

Suddenly Natalia's "powers" were gone. She moved her head in all directions, but she wasn't able to pick the correct words or colors. Defeated, she gave up.

The Verdict

It was all a trick, Randi said. Natalia's nose had an unusual shape that created gaps she could peek through when wearing her own blindfold. "By placing duct tape over the bridge of her nose," Randi explained, "I blocked out her ability to see the cards and colors. I also knew that pulling and rubbing her face would loosen the masking tape. That is why I told Natalia not to rub or pull her face."

Randi's $1 million prize still hasn't been claimed. Any takers?

Even though she was blindfolded, Natalia was able to play tic-tac-toe with her coach.

51

HELP WANTED:
Psychologist

Meet two psychologists who have studied ESP.

Q&A: DR. DARYL J. BEM

Dr. Daryl J. Bem is a professor of psychology at Cornell University in New York. He was skeptical about ESP until the Ganzfeld studies (see page 25) convinced him that it was real.

24/7: What got you interested in parapsychology?

DR. DARYL J. BEM: I've been a performing magician all my life. I specialized in mentalism, which is essentially fake ESP. In the late 1980s, the Parapsychological Association invited me to their annual convention. They wanted to be prepared when studying people who might cheat. [I met] a parapsychologist named Charles Honorton who was conducting the Ganzfeld studies. He asked me to come to his lab to investigate his setup.

24/7: Why did he choose you?

DR. BEM: Because I'm a social psychologist who has done controlled psychological research in the lab and also a magician. So I'd know if people were using tricks to get positive results. I was impressed by what I saw at his lab. I even wrote an article with him about his Ganzfeld research.

24/7: What do you like best about your work?

DR. BEM: I like the mystery of thinking there are things not known to us at the moment and that science can help tackle them.

Q&A: DR. CAROLINE WATT

Dr. Caroline Watt is a psychologist. She is interested in investigating the psychological reasons for people's belief in the paranormal.

24/7: Why did you get into this type of work?

DR. CAROLINE WATT: Scientific curiosity. Lots of people have experiences they interpret as paranormal. I think it's an interesting question as to why they have these experiences and beliefs.

24/7: What training do you need to do research in parapsychology?

DR. WATT: A degree in psychology is probably the best place to start. You need to know how to properly design, conduct, and analyze an experiment.

24/7: What's the most difficult part of your work?

DR. WATT: The small number of parapsychologists worldwide severely limits the ability to do research.

24/7: What's the most surprising thing you've discovered in your research?

DR. WATT: That the beliefs of the experimenter seem to affect the results that they obtain, even under highly controlled conditions.

24/7: What type of person do you think is best suited to do your type of job?

DR. WATT: A patient and intelligent one.

DO YOU HAVE WHAT IT TAKES?

Take this totally unscientific quiz to find out whether being a psychologist might be a good career for you.

1. Are you curious about why people behave the way they do?

a) I always wonder about people and the choices they make.

b) I'm curious about my friends' behavior. Does that count?

c) Not really. I think everybody should mind their own business.

2. Do you think a lot about your own actions and motivations?

a) I agree with the person who said that the unexamined life is not worth living.

b) It's good to give yourself a reality check—every once in a while.

c) People do that? How weird.

3. Do you question the ideas and beliefs you learn about?

a) It's your duty as a thinking being to question things!

b) Up to a point. But you should also just accept some things.

c) I guess I should, but I'm busy just chilling.

4. Are you interested in learning about how the mind works?

a) Of course. The mind is the most amazing thing in the universe.

b) Sure, but isn't that stuff really complicated?

c) I'm more interested in learning how they get the bubbles into soda cans.

5. Do you like the idea of designing and running your own experiments?

a) I love the idea of testing a theory to see whether it's true.

b) As long as I get the results I want! I hate being wrong.

c) That sounds like a lot of work.

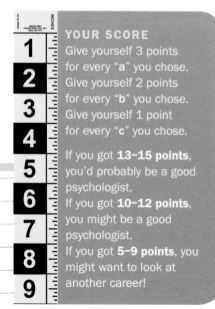

YOUR SCORE

Give yourself 3 points for every "**a**" you chose. Give yourself 2 points for every "**b**" you chose. Give yourself 1 point for every "**c**" you chose.

If you got **13–15 points**, you'd probably be a good psychologist.

If you got **10–12 points**, you might be a good psychologist.

If you got **5–9 points**, you might want to look at another career!

HOW TO GET STARTED...NOW!

It's never too early to start working toward your goals.

GET AN EDUCATION!
▶ Focus on your science, math, and language arts classes.
▶ Look at colleges with good psychology and science departments.
▶ Volunteer to help out at a community or health center, or at a youth or outreach program.
▶ Read anything you can find about psychology. Magazines are filled with interesting stories on psychological topics. See the books and Web sites in the Resources section on pages 56–58.
▶ Graduate from high school!

NETWORK!
Talk to your school psychologist about his or her job. Ask him or her to put you in touch with other people working in the field of psychology, such as counselors and social workers.

GET AN INTERNSHIP
If you live in a college community, contact the psychology department. Ask if they need interns.

LEARN ABOUT OTHER JOBS IN THE FIELD
▶ social worker
▶ sports psychologist
▶ forensic psychologist
▶ clinical psychologist

THE STATS

JOBS: There are few jobs in parapsychology. Most people interested in studying ESP earn their livings as psychologists. Many of them teach at the college level. They do research at university laboratories and write articles and books about their work.

Other psychologists work as **therapists**, helping people with problems. Some work in health, education, or government. A sports psychologist deals with the mental factors that affect an athlete's performance.

MONEY: $40,000–$125,000 per year.

EDUCATION: Jobs in psychology require at least four years of college. People who want to teach or do research need a master's or doctoral degree.

THE NUMBERS: The American Psychological Association has 148,000 members.

Resources

Looking for more mind-expanding information about psychology and parapsychology? Here are some resources you don't want to miss!

PROFESSIONAL ORGANIZATIONS AND WEB SITES

American Psychological Association
www.apa.org
750 First Street, NE
Washington, DC 20002
PHONE: 800-374-2721

This scientific and professional association represents psychology in the United States. It has 148,000 members, making it the largest psychological organization in the world.

American Society for Psychical Research
www.aspr.com/index.html
5 West 73rd Street
New York, NY 10023
PHONE: 212-799-5050

The oldest psychical organization in the United States, the ASPR has a large library in New York City. The society provides its members with journals, newsletters, online research, and updates on important lectures and meetings focusing on the topic of parapsychology.

Association for Psychological Science
www.psychologicalscience.org
1010 Vermont Avenue, NW
11th floor
Washington, DC 20005
PHONE: 202-783-2077

This nonprofit group is dedicated to the advancement of scientific psychology and its representation throughout the United States and the world. It was previously known as the American Psychological Society.

James Randi Educational Foundation
www.randi.org
201 SE 12th Street
Fort Lauderdale, FL 33316
PHONE: 954-467-1112

The goal of this nonprofit organization is to promote critical thinking by providing reliable information about paranormal and supernatural claims.

Parapsychological Association
www.parapsych.org
1390 N. McDowell Blvd.
Suite G-208
Petaluma, CA 94954

This international organization provides its members with a large archive of academic articles, book descriptions, Web forums, experimental data, and photographs.

Parapsychology Foundation, Inc.
www.parapsychology.org
Box 1562
New York, NY 10021

The Parapsychology Foundation is a not-for-profit foundation that provides a worldwide support system for the scientific investigation of psychic phenomena. The foundation holds library collections in New York, publishes the *International Journal of Parapsychology*, hosts lecture series, provides research grants, and much more.

The Rhine Research Center
www.rhine.org
2741 Campus Walk Avenue
Building 500
Durham, NC 27705
PHONE: 919-309-4600

This organization provides courses of study, online message boards, journal articles, and academic writings that all focus on the topic of paranormal consciousness.

BOOKS

Crisp, Tony. *Super Minds: People with Amazing Mind Power*. Rockport, Mass.: Element Books, 1999.

Doherty, Gillian, and Gill Harvey. *The Usborne Book of the Paranormal*. Eveleth, Minn.: Usborne Books, 2000.

Herbst, Judith. *ESP* (The Unexplained). Minneapolis: Lerner, 2004.

Netzley, Patricia. *ESP* (The Mystery Library). Minneapolis: Lerner, 2000.

O'Neill, Terry, ed. *ESP* (Fact or Fiction?). New York: Greenhaven Press, 2002.

Oxlade, Chris. *The Mystery of ESP* (Can Science Solve?). Chicago: Heinemann, 2002.

Randi, James. *Flim-Flam! Psychics, ESP, Unicorns, and Other Delusions*. New York: Prometheus Books, 1982.

Weist-Meyer, Mariam. *Mysteries of the Mind* (Great Unsolved Mysteries). Austin: Steck-Vaughn, 1997.

DVDS

Mysterious Forces Beyond: Psychic Power. Delta, 2002.

This program explores the phenomena of psychic healing, psychic detective work, and channeling.

The Quantum Hologram and ESP. UFO TV, 2005.

Former astronaut Dr. Edgar Mitchell presents a scientific explanation for psychic phenomena.

Remote Viewing & ESP from the Inside Out. UFO TV, 2004.

Introduces viewers to the history and science of the particular form of extrasensory perception known as remote viewing.

The Unexplained: ESP, Dreams, and Disasters. A&E Home Video, 2006.

The stories of four ordinary people predicting inconceivable events.

C

clairvoyance (klair-VOY-uhns) *noun* the ability claimed by some psychics to "see" things beyond the range of normal vision

clairvoyant (klair-VOY-uhnt) *noun* somebody with the supposed ability to "see" things beyond the range of normal vision

convey (kun-VAY) *verb* to communicate something by a suggestion, gesture, or some other means

custody (KUH-stuh-dee) *noun* the legal right to look after a child

D

deduction (dih-DUK-shun) *noun* the use of clues and reasoning to reach a conclusion

E

emigrated (EM-uh-grate-ed) *verb* left one country to live in another

ESP (ee-ess-PEE) *noun* the ability to get information about the past, present, or future without using the five main senses. ESP stands for *extrasensory perception*.

F

frantic (FRAN-tik) *adjective* wild or distraught with fear, anxiety, or another emotion

H

hunches (HUN-chez) *noun* feelings or guesses based on intuition rather than known facts

M

mediums (MEE-dee-uhmz) *noun* people who claim to be able to communicate with the spirits of people who have died

mentalist (MEN-tuh-list) *noun* a performer who uses tricks to make people think he or she has paranormal power, such as the ability to read minds

P

paranormal (PAIR-uh-NOR-muhl) *adjective* a term used to describe unusual events or amazing powers that are beyond scientific explanation

parapsychologists (PAIR-uh-sye-KOHL-uh-jists) *noun* scientists who focus on studying the paranormal

precognition (pree-kog-NIH-shun) *noun* the supposed ability to know about something before it happens—to be able to see into the future

predict (pruh-DIKT) *verb* to say what you think will happen in the future

pseudoscience (SOO-doh-SYE-uhns) *noun* a set of theories that seem to be based on science but that aren't really scientific; *pseudo* means "false."

psychic (SYE-kik) *noun* somebody who claims to have ESP or other paranormal powers

psychokinesis (sye-koh-kih-NEE-sis) *noun* the supposed ability to use the mind to move or change objects; also known as PK

psychologists (sye-KOHL-uh-jists) *noun* scientists who study behavior and the way the mind works

psychology (sye-KOHL-uh-jee) *noun* the study of behavior and how the mind works

S

session (SEH-shun) *noun* a period devoted to a particular activity

sixth sense (sixth sens) *noun* another term for ESP

skeptic (SKEP-tik) *noun* somebody who doubts or questions ideas or beliefs

Spiritualism (speer-ih-choo-wuh-LIH-zuhm) *noun* a system of belief or religious practice based on supposed communication with the spirits of the dead

statisticians (stah-tuh-STIH-shunz) *noun* mathematicians who collect, interpret, and present numerical data

T

telepathy (teh-LEH-puh-thee) *noun* mind reading or mind-to-mind communication through ESP

theory (THEE-uh-ree) *noun* a general idea that explains how or why something happens

therapists (THAIR-uh-pists) *noun* professionals who have been trained to help people who are dealing with mental problems or psychological disorders

Z

Zener cards (ZEE-nur kardz) *noun* a set of 25 cards, each with one of five different symbols, used in ESP research

Stanislawa Tomczyk was a Polish medium who was said to have psychokinesis. This 1913 photo shows her supposedly lifting a pair of scissors without touching them. Some researchers believed her powers were real; others weren't convinced.

Index

Photo Credits: Photographs © 2008: Alamy
Images/Martin Norris: 14; Bridgeman Art Library
International Ltd., London/New York/Private
Collection: 44; CBS Photo Archive: 20, 21;
Courtesy of Committee for Skeptical Inquiry:
6 bottom, 47 bottom; Corbis Images: 40
(Bettmann), 6 top, 47 center (Hulton-Deutsch
Collection), 33 (Michael S. Yamashita), 36 (Vic
Yepello/Star Ledger); Courtesy of Daryl J. Bem:
52; Couresty of Dr. Caroline Watt: 53; Fortean
Picture Library: 5 center, 25, 26, 31; Getty
Images: cover inset (VEER Geoff Graham), 22
(Dave Nagel), cover background (Stockbyte),
47 top (Hank Walker/Time Life Pictures); James
Levin Studios: 4 bottom, 8; Jonathan Saunders:
51 top; JupiterImages: 5 bottom, 39; Library
of Congress/McManus-Young Collection: 46
bottom; Courtesy of Marc Salem: 17, 19; Mary
Evans Picture Library: back cover bottom, back
cover top, 11 top, 11 second from top, 11
center, 11 second from bottom, 11 bottom,
28, 46 top, 61; Courtesy of Nancy Orlen Weber:
37; Photo Researchers, NY/Oscar Burriel: 3;
PhotoEdit/Jeff Greenberg: 34; Retna Ltd.: 48
(Jean/allaction.co.uk), 5 top, 15, 16 (TSPL);
ShutterStock, Inc./Bryan Busovicki: 41; Sipa
Press/Interfoto USA: 1, 2; Superstock, Inc.:
43; The Art Archive/Picture Desk/Ocean
Memorabilia Collection: 49; Courtesy of The
James Randi Educational Foundation: 51
bottom; The Rhine Center: 4 top, 10.
Maps by David Lindroth, Inc.

Writing this book meant that I got to talk to all sorts of cool people including psychics, magicians, psychologists, and parapsychologists.

One memorable discussion I had was with mentalist Marc Salem. Although we talked by phone, I felt totally exposed, like he could see everything I was doing. So I sat up straighter at my computer, paid super-close attention to everything he said, and made sure not to pick my nose! Silly, I know, because he couldn't see me, but it *felt* like he could.

And then this happened: Marc told me to draw a shape within a shape on a piece of paper. Intrigued, I grabbed a pen and did what he'd asked. "You drew a circle inside a triangle," he said. And that was EXACTLY what I had just drawn! How did he know? Now I *was* convinced he could see through the phone!

I collected myself and remembered that Marc had just spent the past half hour explaining how what he does is trickery, that he does *not* read minds.

So let's explore how he guessed my shapes. Marc knows there are certain shapes people are most likely to draw. A circle within a triangle ranks high on that list. It's also possible that he knows that when people are hurried, like I was, there are certain shapes they are most likely to draw. Or maybe Marc inferred from my personality, from the way I spoke and the things I revealed, that I would most likely draw these two common shapes. (For instance, if I were quirky, he might have deduced I would draw something less common, like a star within a rectangle.)

But I still couldn't shake the feeling that what Marc does is otherworldly, magical. Which is how he manages to awe audiences worldwide. He sure had me mystified!

ACKNOWLEDGMENTS

I would like to thank the following people. I couldn't have written this book without their help:

Marc Salem
Uri Geller
Nancy Weber
Dr. Caroline Watt
Dr. Daryl J. Bem
Jeffrey Nelson
James Randi
Dr. Sally Rhine Feather
Dr. John Palmer

CONTENT ADVISER: Stanley Krippner, PhD, Professor of Psychology, Saybrook Graduate School, San Francisco